Rooms Remembered

Published by Sungold Editions
www.sungoldeditions.com
Book design by Chryss Yost

Cover image:
Detail from "LAMENT," sculpture by Nancy A. Gifford,
used with permission of the artist.
Photographed by Joanne A. Calitri

ISBN-13: 978-0-9991678-1-6

Rooms Remembered

Poem by

Laure-Anne Bosselaar

Sungold Editions • Santa Barbara
2018

Contents

Contents

I needed, for months after he died, to remember our rooms —
  some lit by the trivial, others ample with an obscurity

that comforted us: it hid our own darkness.
  So for months, duteous, I remembered:

rooms where friends lingered, rooms with our beds,
  with our books, rooms with curtains I sewed

from bright cottons. Tables of laughter,
  a chipped bowl in early light, black

branches by a window, bowing toward night, & those rooms,
  too, in which we came together

to be away from all—& sometimes from ourselves:
  I remembered that, also.

But tonight— as I lean into the doorway to his room
  & stare at dusk settled there—

what I remember best is how, to throw my arms around his neck,
  I needed to stand on the tips of my toes.

This longing for him, the choke in my throat again —
　　　　　　　enough, enough.

I throw a coat over my shoulders,
　　　　　　　close the door behind me, softly,

as if afraid to wake another ache.
　　　　　　　Another dawn. It'll seep into the sky

behind the palms. Fists in my pockets, I head east
　　　　　　　into this street

of bungalows as if I belonged here, among the hundred
　　　　　　　windows lit one by one, among the first

joggers & their dogs, past garages yawning out
　　　　　　　cars into the noisy busyness of day.

This longing, again for him, who —
　　　　　　　that June — did not wait for light,

turned his face away from the window &, quietly,
　　　　　　　entered silence.

I heard

    how silence swallowed his last breath —

       & followed him

          inside the silence after that.

Arroyo Burro Beach. The tide dies a while
　　　　　then starts its way up again —
　　　　　　　& up again.

Fog rolls in, dense & sudden. Behind me
　　　　　there's a rock halfway to the end
　　　　　　　of the bay, hunched,

split in two, black & blue with mussels —

　　　　　that's where I turn around & walk
back each day. A restlessness
　　　　　swells inside the tides there —

& it's there each time, just before I can look
　　　　　away — then, everything drowns
　　　　　　　into itself again & into gray.

I no longer pick up shells — I let them be:
　　　　　waves rake them back & place them
　　　　　　　at my feet again anyway:

small skeletons, dead, but pretty.

Look at me, writing circles around what I must face:
       The man I love is dead.

The ashes he asked I lose to this ocean are still
             in our room, in a red box
    he gave me, for some birthday, in New York.

His dust. I'll keep it a while longer — I'll keep it

        as one secretly keeps something
            for one's self
& won't, today at least,
           lose more of him to these waves.

Clouds heave over the mountains, rip
          & rain — at last. Years of drought,
               yet spring drenches everything
with jasmine stars & citrus blooms.

The hummingbirds are drunk. All night,
          the mockingbird. Each dawn
the call & call of crows.

      (Tomorrow, his widow for five years.)

At first, no tears. Everything I was told
          would happen as I mourned,
      didn't. No sobs, no rage,
              no stage one, two, three.
No welcome dreams in which he'd appear.

          His cat mourned better than I, lying
on her side for weeks across his room's threshold,
          stretched as much as she could,
              back paws against one side
of the doorjamb, front paws to the other.

She waited for him. I paced the house, the streets.
      No tears. I cleaned & sewed
           & raked & wrote. Sat in the jacaranda's
shade, as its shadow soaked the orchard.

         Walked the beach. Stooped for stones —
how they'd huddle in my palm: a white one tarred black,
      the one like a fist,
         & another with a hole bored
            straight through its center.

I threw them back. The metaphors too blatant.

Nights, I'd walk from the kitchen to the orchard
      & measure it, one foot in front of the other,
         head bent, toes to heel, heel to toes,
           whispering numbers.

         Thirty-four feet wide.
         Thirty-three feet deep.

And still, no tears.

There was a room in Antwerp I loved so much
     I never filled it with books, a bed, or a table.
  It was alive with its own clarity — & I feared
anything left there would etch shadows in that radiance.

The room was in the attic of a hundred-year-old house.
    Hunched under a mansard roof, all its windows
faced the sky. No horizon, no walls, no other windows
      stared into mine.

The wide-planked floor had been painted over for more
    than a century. Scratches in the floor revealed other
      colors under its white surface. A deep scuff
showed a reddish gray, other scratches yellow, green, or black.

     The sun splashed into that room at noon:
cascades of light. Dust, sucked upward by the heat,
    fluttered under the skylight's chicken-wire glass.
I'd stretch out my palms to the rays then,

        & grab that light, lay on my back & listen —
through the layers of whirling air — to the city's guttural chatter,
the clang of tramways, & melancholic calls of tall ships
                with their crowns of shrieking gulls.

        I owned that light — alive in my hands.

So, how are you? friends ask, all kindness & concern,
                heads cocked, eyes locked in mine.

&, just like that, I'm *his* again:
                his wife, his widow: the one whose name

was hyphenated to his — & I'm oddly
                happy to speak about

myself, coupled to him again, finally,
                & say I'm *okay, better*, but won't say his name

out loud yet because I know
                I'd throw a shadow over the conversation —

all kindness & concern — & over him also,
                who no longer has a shadow.

The empty room I loved led to a larger one, where I lived.

On the floor, by my bed, askew on a stack of books,
        stood my small transistor radio. It caught
                three stations:

                One was a pirate radio, broadcasting
from a ship in the North Sea.
        The other, with Flemish news, only came on
                two hours each night, & the one I listened to
        most was a classical music station.

It played, uninterrupted, for an hour or more,
        then, after a minute or two of absolute silence,
            a woman's exhausted voice.
She must have been in her late eighties
                & constantly stumbled
on musicians' names. I can still hear her say
                "*Rack*-mun-num-nee-*noff.*"

Every hour, the Cathedral of Our Lady chimed a while —

then the treble bell rang the hour.
           I'd stand on a chair, lean through
                    a dormer window to watch
how Our Lady's steeple pierced the light.

Summer of '63. I was free, I was twenty.
           I fell wholly &
           forever in love every week.
                    I was hungry for life

        & satiated by it,
                reading deep into the night, & copied
Sartre, de Beauvoir, Apollinaire, Gide, Rilke,
                    Baudelaire, Senghor, Goethe,
        Rimbaud, & Lorca in my notebooks —

        barely sleeping before I rushed
down to work, then ran back
                up the five steep flights
                    to that white, lit room.

I was twenty then & remember how in stores,
    tramways or cafés, I'd catch someone's gaze,
eyes that took me in &
     held me there
    for an instant. The glint of those stares —
a flash of mica — offered to me & just like that,
      my loneliness
         shattered:
  Everything was light: those eyes, that gaze —

then, just as sudden, I
     disappeared again
  inside the dismissal
     of a blink.

I'd search again & again for other eyes, other heart-
    gasping moments to take me in, hold me —
it didn't matter how briefly
     as long as
     I was held.

(And yet, with him, when — from across a crowd, table, or pillow — his gaze took me in — it was I who looked away first. Oh, always.)

Some nights, settled against him, my face in his neck, I missed him — feeling that he was elsewhere.

I bought a new bed after he died, his imprint in ours unbearable — now that he was nowhere.

How can I say this, if not in the simplest way
     (I had planned to tell him):

Often, I loved to hear — no, *listen to*— his sleeve's
shush on our table.

Some evenings, he would hide his face in his hands
          for a few seconds —

then let go of his held breath
                    & lift his head again, his eyes bereaved
of light.

          What room, face, gaze haunted him?

& where you are, friend, in

          Kansas
          Utah
          Rhode Island
          Tennessee —

what haunts *you*? What is it you choke
inside your palms?

Have you told someone? Have you? Will you?

I had weeded, hemmed, counted,
raked, cleaned. I had written
myself reminders: I needed
to wash the curtains. I had
a knot of nettles in my throat,
I couldn't swallow. *Swallow,
swallow*, I'd say aloud.
     I was asleep when he died.
     I did not wake when he died.
I stood in his orchard. Heard
the wind stuff night into the tree.
I thought of his clothes. I had
stuffed them in a plastic bag &
vacuumed the air out of it:
I had sucked *his air* out of his clothes.
I walked to Las Positas Road,
to Peregrina Street, to Pueblo.
From Pueblo up to Stanley,
back to Las Positas. I remembered
to wash the curtains. I remembered
to feed the cats.

     I was asleep when he died.
     I did not wake when he died.
I broke a dish he loved. I had
filled it with water for the birds.
Four years of drought & the birds
were dying — the hills too. No
clouds. California was burning.
I turned off the radio, hearing this.
I squeezed my thumbs in my fists.
     I was asleep when he died.
I had to go, I had to leave —
I couldn't remember for what.
I couldn't remember for where.
I drove North on the 101, in the dark,
to Refugio Beach.

I listened to Dylan:
She left with the man
with the long black coat.
I made a U-turn —
     I did not wake when he died.

The mountains are
filled with lost sheep.
I counted the cars I passed
(fifty two, plus seventeen
trucks & a bus) drove past
our house to Stella's Café:
He loved to go there
for Happy Hour, he & I
loved to walk there,
he & I, we'd —

       & then — there,
       sudden in Stella's
       parking lot,
the tears.

Horse-hooves, Flemish jabber, & tugboat hoots
ruffle the air. A Sunday in summer. The skylight is open,
        so are the windows. The transistor crackles a piano piece.

I sit in the lit room, by the door, my back to the white
        brick wall — & layer by layer by layer, peel
                away the floor paint in a corner of the threshold.

Paint petals in my palms. A hundred
years of lives, a hundred keys to this door: a thousand
        kisses under the chicken wire skylight, a century
                of slammed doors, baby's cries.

Women, men, couples moving in, choosing
                a color for the floor. Moving out,
        leaving scuffs & scars behind.

The color gray was for a stevedore I knew
        who read North Sea clouds better than God, but couldn't
read or write.

The blue for a boy thumbing his marbles
in the grooves between the planks.

Green for the lovers who rushed upstairs, laughing, breathless,
then walked back down so silently.

But the black paint? The black for the sirens of May 1940.

Hitler's *Blitzkrieg* blanket-bombing Antwerp —
his *Luftwaffe* ordered to
avoid Our Lady by all means:
Hitler loved her: he wanted her for his *Reich*.

Then this thin layer — a dusty yellow.

For the Jews.
It can only be for the Jews.

For their yellow armbands under black Stars of David.
For the Jews cattled to the *Breendonck Transit Camp*

sorted, separated,
beaten, starved, shot

in *Breendonck*: only 14 miles
away from my white, lit room.

Dusk at the end of the old stone pier. Pelicans dive
        deep into the waves as we had into each other.

I stand here, remembering that, but can't
        remember his body's weight on mine.

That man I knew by body & skin & belly & heart —
        I have — so soon — forgotten his weight on me.

Then, you stop weeping. Lift your face from your hands.
       Not because you're done or because it helped,
               but because there's a faint knock at the window.

You look up. It's a branch. It taps & waves & distracts
       your sorrow. You wipe your face
               hard with both hands.

This is not a sign. You're ruefully aware of that, & don't
       believe in signs. They announced a storm,
               it nears, that's all.

Yet the sky is so still — so lit. Again, those knocks
       at the window. It's not him.
               Of course it isn't.

For weeks now, no nettles in my throat.

I clean & count & sew & write & rake.

I walk the ocean's hem & hum a little.

I pick up stones, bring them home: one

tarred black, one with a hole in its center.

I sit by the jacaranda, hold stones in my lap.

I'm cold. It's late, the sun fades,

but just before it turns its back to me,

it wraps a ray around my shoulders, finds

my hands & warms them: weighted,

worn, old, open & lit.

For Kurt

1944-2013

Laure-Anne Bosselaar is the author of *The Hour Between Dog and Wolf*, *Small Gods of Grief*, winner of the Isabella Gardner Prize, and of *A New Hunger*, selected as a Notable Book by the American Library Association. The editor of four anthologies and the recipient of a Pushcart Prize, she teaches at the Solstice Low Residency MFA Program at Pine Manor College. Her next book, *These Many Rooms*, will be published by Four Way Books in early 2019.

Lightning Source UK Ltd.
Milton Keynes UK
UKHW05f2121020418
320416UK00013B/786/P